Learning Sverchok

Parametric and computational design tool for Blender

INDEX

Note about Blender's version:

This book has been written using Blender 2.79 and Sverchok 0.5.9.6. At the time of writing, Blender 2.80 it's in its beta phase. As soon as the stable version of Blender 2.80 will be released, the book will be updated. If you want to use already Blender 2.80, most of the Sverchok features presented in this edition should look and work the same and the same principles apply.

INTRODUCTION

Why this book

This short book is born with the intent of providing people a **solid understanding** of the basic knowledge necessary to use proficiently Sverchok, Blender's node-based parametric design add-on.

Parametric design is getting more and more popular, yet most of the tools dedicated to this field are part of highly priced software packages like Rhino/Grasshopper. Sverchok offers a valid alternative for students, small businesses and hobbyists that are interested in this fascinating field. The fact that Sverchok comes as an add-on to Blender, with direct access to all its **powerful Python API** makes things even more exciting.

Since a tool like Sverchok is closer to a **programming language** than to a traditional 3D modeling environment, some basic concepts and rules have to be clear and defined. This book tries to give you this knowledge, besides offering an overview of the major Sverchok functionalities. At the end of the read you will have what it takes to start exploring Sverchok independently and to start using it to realize your **amazing ideas**.

Things you should know before starting

A **basic knowledge of Blender** is assumed. General Blender structure, navigating and changing the interface, basic commands and operations in the *3D view* and in the *Outliner* are all things you should already be familiar with as they will be given for granted.

You should know the **basics of vector math and trigonometry**, since these are two fields that are used extensively in computational design. If your knowledge of these two topics is 0, I recommend to look at the dedicated lectures on websites like Khan academy before starting, it will not take you much more than an hour to get the informations necessary to follow proficiently this course.

A basic **experience with programming** is not necessary but if you have one it's definitely an advantage. Anyway any programming-related topic will be explained starting from the basics.

Book structure

The book provides with all the knowledge necessary to use Sverchok with a solid grounding and without incurring into too many frustrations. That's why, after setting up the environment in Blender (chapter 1 - "**Setting up the environment**"-), in the chapter 2 - "**Sverchok basics**" - we explain in detail the data structures of Sverchok before moving our first steps into the add-on. Chapter 3 - "**Problem setting and solving in computational design**" - discusses from a theoretical and a practical standpoint how you should face the solution of a computational design problem. After having built this solid grounding, in chapter 4 - "**Monads and presets**" - we discover two useful features of Sverchok. Chapter 5 - "**Matrices**" - and 6 - "**Logic**" - address two slightly more complex topics that nevertheless are crucial in our context. Finally, chapter 7 - "**Intro to Python components**" - provides a brief overview of how you can boost your Sverchok potential using Python.

About me

My name is **Alberto Maria Giachino**, I have a master degree in Urban Planning from the *Politecnico di Torino*. After my graduation I discovered a passion for programming and now I am working in this field as one of the developers of Voxelizer, a slicer for FDM and DLP 3D printers. These interests of mine for coding, digital fabrication, forms and design led me first to start the Creative Coding meetup in the city of Wrocław, where I am based, and then to start my blog Code Plastic (www.codeplastic.com) where I talk about all these topics. In the meantime I discovered Blender and Sverchok, that I keep learning and exploring.

1. SETTING UP THE ENVIRONMENT

In this chapter we will see how to install Sverchok and how to set up our Blender environment for parametric design. We will also see where we can find useful resources regarding Sverchok.

1.1 Installing Sverchok

You can install Sverchok just like any other Blender add-on. First download the Sverchok zip file at https://github.com/nortikin/sverchok/archive/master.zip, then go to *File→User Preferences→Add-ons→Install Add-on from File...* and select what you have just downloaded. Then once it is installed look for it in the list under *"Node:Sverchok"* and tick the flag to activate it.

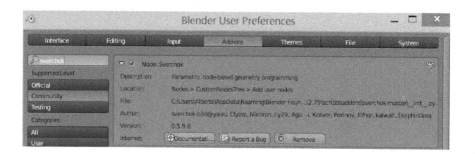

You will find Sverchok in the *Node Editor* under the icon that resemble the DNA helix. Enable it permanently by pressing CTRL+U→*Save startup file*.

1.2 Sverchok resources

Here is a list of places you can refer to when looking for documentation, help, tutorials or inspiration:

- https://sverchok.readthedocs.io/en/latest/main.html   The official Sverchok documentation. Here you will find a description of most of the nodes that are present, plus some tutorials.
- https://github.com/nortikin/sverchok The official Sverchok GitHub repository. Here you can download the latest release of Sverchok, look at the source code, read the wiki. The *Issues* page (https://github.com/nortikin/sverchok/issues) is also a sort of forum for the community, where you can report bugs but also make questions and share your results and ideas.
- http://nikitron.cc.ua/sverchok_en.html   The Sverchok website from its creator, in English and Russian. Here you can find various tutorials, links and resources.
- https://plus.google.com/communities/11324523101315949 7850 and https://vk.com/public35076122 the Google+ and VK (in Russian) groups, for news and inspiration.
- https://blendersushi.blogspot.com/   and https://www.youtube.com/channel/UC7ED1eB6DET3fPOW xcDJ1lw Jimmy Gunawan blog and his YouTube channel are a super resource, full of tutorials and videos about Sverchok.
- http://www.codeplastic.com My blog, with tutorials for Sverchok and other computational design related articles.

1.3 Setting up Blender for parametric design

This step is not mandatory, however I recommend you to create a new **Screen layout dedicated to parametric design**. Here is how I do it.

After activating Sverchok from the *User Preferences*, In the *Info* editor's header click on the + icon to *Add a new screen*. We can call it *"Parametric design"*.

I suggest **organizing it in this way**: change the *Timeline* to the **Node Editor**, make it occupy approximately half of the screen in height and select the Sverchok icon; next to the *3D view* add a **Text editor**, it will be important when we will be debugging Sverchok's programs; if you want now you can remove the default cubes, camera and light and press *CTRL+U→Save Startup File* so that the next time that you will open Blender you will find the same setup.

Now you are ready to go!

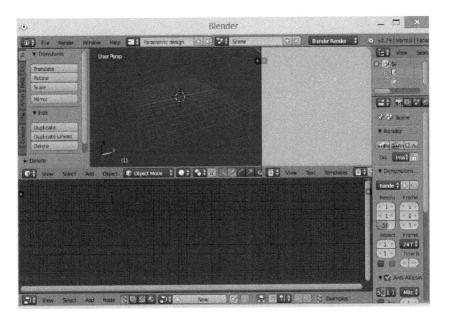

2. SVERCHOK BASICS

In the first part of this chapter we will understand how the geometry is represented inside of Sverchok and how we can manipulate it. Then we will have our first encounter with nodes and we will look at the Sverchok interface.

2.1 Vertices, Edges and Polygons and Sverchok Data structure

Before moving into Blender and starting to do our first experiments with parametric modeling, it is a good idea to have a good understanding of **how the geometry is represented in Sverchok**, so that later on we can easily manipulate it.

Let's see, for example, how we can **represent a cube**.

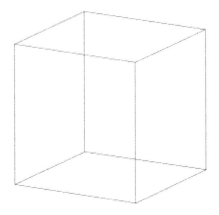

2.1.1. Vertices, Edges and Polygons

The fundamental elements of the geometry are the **vertices**. Vertices are **3D vectors** with an x, y, z component, representing their position on the three Cartesian axes. For example we will have the vertex A at position $(0,5,1)$.

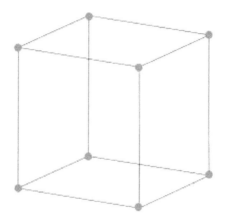

Then we have the **edges**. Each edge is described by two vertices. For example we will have the edge *a* made by the vertices A and B.

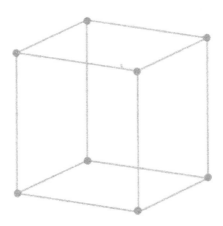

Finally, we have **polygons**. Each polygon is described by at least 3 edges and, as a consequence, by at least three vertices. For example we will have the polygon A made the vertices ABCD.

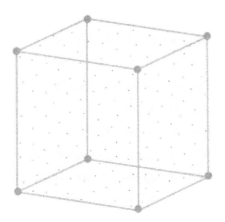

2.1.2 Lists

Inside of Sverchok, all the elements previously described are stored into *lists*. Lists are data structures, containers where you can store data. Inside of Python, the programming language that Sverchok is using, a list is represented by **two squared brackets**. The items stored in the lists are called *elements*. We can imagine, for example, a list called "fruits_list" that contains three elements: "orange", "apple" and "banana". It will look like this:

```
fruits_list = ["orange", "apple", "banana"]
```

Lists offer fast and ordered storage. We can quickly access the elements of a list by their *index*. The index is an integer (non decimal) number that go from zero to the number of elements inside the list minus one. In our previous example "orange", being the first element of the list, has index 0, "apple" 1 and "banana" 2. As you can see "banana", the last element of the list, has an index equal to the number of elements inside the list (three) minus one. To retrieve an element from a list using its index we also use square brackets, in this way:

```
fruits_list[0] #This corresponds to "orange"
fruits_list[1] #This corresponds to "apple"
fruits_list[2] #This corresponds to "banana"
```

When you will be debugging Sverchok, instead of squared brackets you could see rounded brackets. Here the data structure used is not a list but a *tuple*. In Python, tuples differ from lists in the fact that they are unchangeable, meaning that once a tuple has been created, it cannot be modified. You don't have to worry about this anyway, because in Sverchok the two data structures are treated basically in the same way and you can consider them equivalent. Just know that you might encounter something like this:

```
fruits_tuple = ("kiwi", "pineapple", "avocado")
fruits_tuple[1] #This corresponds to "pineapple"
```

2.1.3 Vertex list

Vertices, for example, are usually (but not necessarily) represented using tuples:

```
a_vertex = (23.5, 1.0, 3.2)
```

23.5 is the position of the vertex on the x axis, 1.0 on the y axis and 3.2 on the z axis. To retrieve a component of its location we will then do in this way:

```
z_position = a_vertex[2]
```

We can also encapsulate lists and tuples one inside the others, depending on our needs. In fact, now that we know about these two data structures, we can go back to our cube and see how we can use them to describe it in Sverchok.

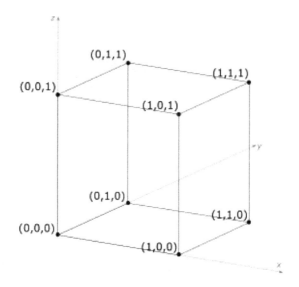

As we have seen, the vertices are the foundations, that's why we will create at first the **vertex list**.

```
vertex_list = [ (0,0,0), (0,1,0), (1,1,0), (1,0,0),
(0,0,1), (0,1,1), (1,1,1), (1,0,1) ]
```

2.1.4. Edge list

Then we will have the **edge list**. As we know an edge is described by two vertices; in Sverchok we represent an edge with a two-elements list containing the indices of its vertices inside the vertex list.

```
an_edge = [0,1]
```

In our example, `an_edge` is made by the vertices that in `vertex_list` have index 0 and 1, namely the two vertices at position (0,0,0) and (0,1,0).
The edge list will then look this:

```
edge_list = [ [0,1], [1,2], [2,3], [3,0], [0,4],
[1,5], [3,7], [2,6], [4,5], [5,6], [6,7], [7,4] ]
```

2.1.5. Polygon list

The **polygons** are like edges. They are lists containing lists of the indices of the vertices making the polygon. If you have a polygon, then implicitly you already have the edges.

```
a_polygon = [0,3,2,1]
```

We can now write the **polygon list**, in this way completing the information that we need to represent a geometry in Sverchok.

```
polygon_list = [ [0,3,2,1], [0,1,5,4], [1,2,6,5],
[2,6,7,3], [0,3,7,4], [4,7,6,5] ]
```

Now that we have the vertex list, the edge list and the polygon list we can correctly represent our cube inside of Sverchok.

2.1.6. Levels and objects

Before moving forward, few important notes about lists: we have already seen how we can have lists (or tuples) inside of lists (or tuples). This process can go on almost indefinitely and a single list can have many *levels* of encapsulation.

```
one_level_list = [ 3,5,6 ]
two_levels_list = [ [ 4,1,0 ], [ 2,1 ] ]
three_levels_list = [ [ [4,6 ], [ 4 ] ], [ [ 3,4 ]
] ]
```

We start counting the levels from 0, where the level 0 is the list itself and then incrementing the count as we go "deeper" inside of it.

```
three_levels_list = [ [ [4,6], [ 4 ] ], [ [ 3,4 ] ]
]
```

In Sverchok the elements contained at the level 0 are called *objects*: two_levels_list has two objects, one_level_list has three objects. This might not look important now, but it will become later on, when we will have to debug our node trees. Take for example these two lists:

```
list_a = [ [ 5,6,7 ], [ 7,2,1 ] ]
list_b = [ [ [ 5,6,7 ], [ 7,2,1 ] ] ]
```

Although they contain the same values, the two lists are not equal because they don't have the same structure. `list_a` contains two objects, `list_b` one object. In Sverchok sometimes you need to pass data that have a specific structure (for example a list containing just a single object), or if you have multiple inputs you cannot pass lists that contain a different number of objects or that don't have the same amount of levels. On top of that, some nodes in Sverchok modify the data structure of your inputs. For example you pass a list with this structure [[x,y,z]] and as an output you get a list with this structure [[[x,y,z]]]. Both lists contain one object but the first one has two levels, the second one three. This might produce problems and frustrations if you are not aware of these kinds of situations.

It is important that you have clear the content of this chapter. Being able to read, understand and debug the content of lists is an essential skill inside of Sverchok, if you don't want to spend hours trying to figure out why your node tree doesn't want to work.

2.1.7. Exercise

To conclude, try this **exercise**. Take this pyramid and write the vertex list, the edge list and the polygon list and make sure that each contains only one object.

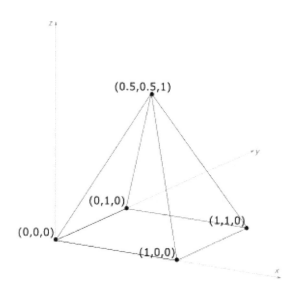

vertex_list = [[(0,0,0) '(1,0,0) '(1,1,0) '(0,1,0) '(0.5,0.5,1)]]]
edge_list = [[[0,1] '[1,2] '[2,3] '[3,0] '[0,4] '[1,4] '[2,4] '[3,4]]]
polygon_list = [[[0,1,2,3] '[0,1,4] '[1,2,4] '[2,3,4] '[3,0,4]]]]

2.2 Hello Sverchok

Now that we know how Sverchok represents geometry, we can start to get our feet wet by creating **our first node tree**. The first thing that you do when you learn a new programming language is creating an **"Hello World"** program. Since Sverchok is comparable to a programming language, a graphical/node-based one, we will also write our "Hello World", or "Hello Sverchok", if you will.

2.2.1 Creating a new node tree

To work with Sverchok, as we said, we need to be inside of the *Node Editor*, having the Sverchok icon selected. Now we have an empty canvas, however we cannot work with it yet, first we need to **create a new node tree**. We can do this by clicking on the + New button.

Now that we have a node tree we can change its name. Click on "*NodeTree*", write "*Hello Sverchok*" and press *Enter*.

2.2.2 Adding nodes to the node tree

Now we can start to **add nodes**. To do this we have three options, my favorite is pressing *SHIFT + A* on the main area. A list with all the nodes categories will appear. Don't worry about them now, we will explore them during the course. By clicking on a category a list of the available nodes will appear (or other sub-categories).

By clicking on a node, this will be added to the layout. You will notice that there is also a **Search** option in the list, where you can look for a node directly with its name (you can use this function directly also by pressing *CTRL + SPACEBAR* in the main area). This is quick and practical, however at the beginning I recommend you not to use this feature and instead to search manually through the nodes categories. In this way you will get more familiar with the names and you will discover by yourself new interesting nodes.

Now, try to add the Box node from the *Generator* category and Viewer Draw from *Viz*, we will work with them soon.

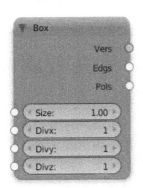 

Another way to add nodes to the layout is clicking on *Add*, in the header. The same nodes categories with the related nodes will show up and you can select what you need from here as well. Finally, in the *Tool Shelf*, you will find the node that you need in one of the tabs, each corresponding to a category (except the first two, that we will cover in another chapter).

2.2.3. Input and output sockets

Great, now we have our first two nodes. You can **select** them by left-clicking on them and you can **drag** them around by dragging them with the left mouse or by pressing *G* after selection.

Each node performs something different, allowing you to create, analyze and modify geometry and data. The `Box` node for example will create a box geometry and `Viewer Draw` will render it in the *3D view*. As you might have notice though, at the moment you don't see any cube anywhere: stay with me.

Each node has always some **input or output sockets**, or both of the two. The **inputs** are the data necessary for the node to perform its specific actions, the **outputs** are its results. If a node doesn't have enough inputs to perform its task, it will stay idle and/or will become orange; if it gets the wrong ones, it will raise an error and will become red. The inputs are normally numeric data in the form of lists (but not always). The outputs can either be data or some type of action: this is the case of the `Viewer Draw`, for example, that will render the geometry in the *3D View, whereas* the `Box` node takes data as input and provides other data as output. When it comes to input parameters, depending on the node, you can either input directly the data or link the output sockets of some other nodes, or both of the two (like in the case of the Box).

To link two sockets, simply drag the mouse from to another.

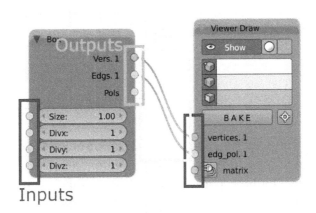

Inputs

In our case, try to link the Vers socket in the Box with the vertices' socket in the Viewer Draw and Edgs with edg_pol. A cube will appear in the 3D view! Congratulation, your first working Sverchok node tree! We have finally written our "Hello Sverchok". Now we can say that a **node tree** is a set of nodes linked together that produces a sensible output.

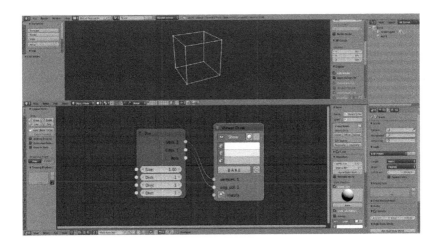

Let's analyze a bit more what we have in front of us, particularly regarding input and output sockets. There are **four types of sockets**: orange for the vertices (v), blue for the matrices (m), green for strings and lists (s) and gray for the objects (o).

In most of the cases, you can only **link sockets of the same type**. When you try to link sockets of different types or you provide incorrect data formats (say, a list of lists instead of a simple list) you can have different situations: Sverchok could show you clearly that there is an error by turning one or more nodes red, or you might get some strange and unexpected results, or the node tree could be stuck in the last valid output. Try for example to link Edgs to matrix and you will see what I am talking about.

2.2.4. Reading lists content

Now that we know the rules of the game, let's try to move a little bit forward. For example, let's see if what we said in the previous part about Sverchok data structure is correct. We will start by adding a new node, Viewer Index from *Viz*. Now Link Vers with Vertices. The **indices of the vertex list** of the cube will appear in the *3D view*. If you cannot see them clearly, click on the *Background* button inside the node. Now that we know which position each vertex occupies inside the vertex list, we will keep it as a reference while we investigate the three output lists of the Box node.

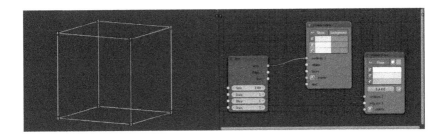

Now we need a way to **inspect the content of lists**. The easiest options is the Stethoscope MK2 node, under *Text*.

Add it and link Vers from Box to Data. You will see how the data are structured and you will notice that they are like how we described them in the previous chapter. Check also the edge list and of the polygon list.

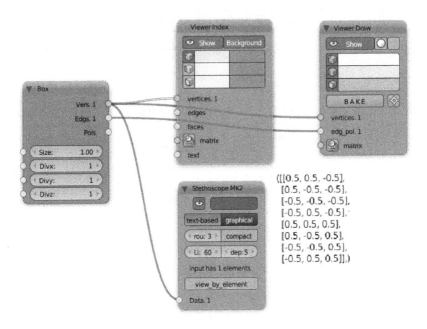

Another way to inspect the content of a list (which I prefer) is to use the Viewer Text MK3 node, also under *Text*. I recommend the following setup: check the autoupdate parameter and uncheck the frame one; next to the *3D view* create a new area and set it to be a *Text editor;* if you have already linked the data socket with an input (for example the vertex list of the cube) and clicked on the *VIEW* button you will see that in the available files of the *Text editor* there is one called **Sverchok_viewer;** select it and you will find the data formatted and organized in a readable way. Try to link the edges and the polygon list and make sure you find correspondence with what we have seen in the previous chapter.

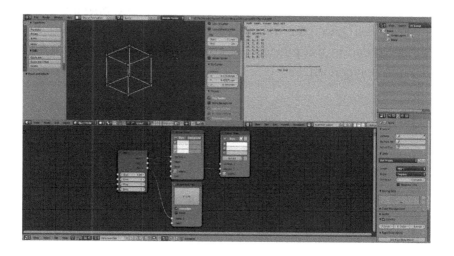

The three nodes that we have just seen Viewer Index, Stethoscope MK2 and Viewer Text MK3 are your allies in times of debugging, get familiar with them!

2.2.5. Baking

Before concluding this lesson, one last element: now we have created our cube and we can see it. However, maybe we would like to export it, or to add it to other assets that we have created in the *3D view* or perform some other type of actions not possible in Sverchok. At the moment we cannot do any of this. The solution is to **bake** the cube and we can do this simply by clicking *BAKE* in the `Viewer Draw`. Now we have a new object in the *3D view* that also appears in the *Outliner*. This object is not related anymore with Sverchok, so if we modify our cube in Sverchok the changes will not be reflected in the object previously created.

Another option that will generate directly an asset immediately available in the *Outliner*, while keeping the connection with the Sverchok node tree, is the `Viewer BMesh` from *Viz*. One of the advantages of this node is that you can, for example, apply modifiers from the *Properties* while keep editing the shape in the node tree. If I don't need to do something like this though, I tend to prefer the `Viewer Draw` as it allows me to control more easily the visualization of vertices, edges and polygons.

2.2.6. Exercise

Get familiar with the other generators, like `Plane`, `Circle` or `Cylinder`. Play with them and analyze their lists.

2.3 Sverchok interface

In this chapter we will have a general look at **Sverchok interface**. We will go into the details, where necessary, during the rest of the course. It's a bit of a documentation-style chapter and not very exciting, but I advise to read it to have a general understanding of the Sverchok features.

2.3.1 Adding and browsing through nodes

We already know that to **create** a new node tree we need to click on the *New* button in the header of the *Node editor*. Once a node tree is created we can easily **change its name**. Create a node tree and call it "Useful node tree". You can create and **add** to your blend file as many node trees as you want, just click on the + icon, near the name of your current node tree. Try it. You will have a new empty area. Call it "Useless node tree". By clicking on the Sverchok icon with the two arrow you will be able to **browse** between all your node trees. Go back to "Useful node tree".

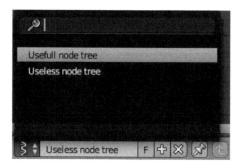

2.3.2. Deleting node trees

Let's see how we can **delete** a node tree that we don't need.

Maybe you are already familiar with the concept of **data-blocks**, if not, you need to know that Blender organizes the content of each blend file in data-blocks. Data-blocks are the base units for any Blender project. Examples of data-blocks include: meshes, objects, materials, textures, scenes, texts, brushes... Node trees are another type of data-block. Each data-block has a certain number of "users" which represent the number of links the data-block has to other data-blocks i.e. from how many meshes one material is used. If a data-block has zero users at the moment of closing a file, Blender will delete it. This is a way to keep under control the size of Blender files.

The best way to delete a node tree from Sverchok, if we want to, is to **set its number of users to zero**. We can do this by pressing the *x* icon while holding SHIFT. This forces the user count of the node-tree to zero. Now we can save the file and the next time that you will open it you will not find the node tree that had zero users. Alternatively, after you have saved your file, you can go to *file->revert*, which does the same thing described before in place.

Another option is, after setting the number of users of the node tree to zero, then temporary change the node editor to the *3d view* and in the *tool shelf* find the **Sverchok panel,** where you will find all your node-tree. If you click on *Clean layouts,* the node-trees with zero users will be removed.

2.3.3. *Node editor* header

Let's go now through each part of the Sverchok interface and see what we can find, starting from the header. Sverchok is not the only node editor in Blender, although it's the only for parametric design, and the *Node editor* header is common to all of them. Some elements are in common and some are not. Let's look at them, moving left to right.

- **View**: different functions related to the visualization of the node tree. *View all* is particularly useful, with his *home* key shortcut. Try it. Here you can also activate the *tool shelf* and the *properties* region which we will cover in a moment.
- **Select**: different functions for selecting the nodes. As you can see the familiar *B* and *C* and other types of selection are available.
- **Add**: lets you add nodes from the various categories to the current node tree.

- **Node**: different useful functions related to the selected nodes. We will cover some of them while we proceed with the course.
- **Node tree type selector**: Here you can switch to other node editors.
- **Browse node tree** and **New button**: covered in the previous paragraphs.
- **Use the pinned node tree**: related to other node editors and not to Sverchok.
- **Go to parent node tree**: same as point before.
- **Offset**: from Blender docs: "When you drop a node with at least one input and one output socket onto an existing connection between two nodes, Auto-offset will, depending on the direction setting, automatically move the left or right node away to make room for the new node. Auto-offset is a feature that helps organizing node layouts interactively without interrupting the user workflow."
- **Snap**: if selected, it will snap the nodes to the grid or to other nodes, depending on the value setted in the next drop-down list. Personally, I prefer to have this off but you can give it a try and decide by yourself.
- **Copy** and **paste**: allows you to copy and paste the selected nodes. Note: **works only between the same blender file**. To copy nodes to another files you will have to do in the way that we will describe soon.
- **Examples**: here you will find different examples of node-trees created by the developers of Sverchok. They are a great source of inspiration and learning. You can start to check them and see if you can make sense of what is going on.

2.3.4. Tool shelf

To conclude, let's look at the two side regions of the *Node Editor*, the *tool shelf* and the *properties*. In the **tool shelf** you will find all the Sverchok nodes subdivided by categories. As we have seen this is another way to **insert nodes** inside the tree although personally I never use it. At the top of the *tool shelf* there is the **grease pencil** tab. This is a way to take notes in the main area that could eventually be transformed into geometry; anyway we will not use it and due to that we can skip it.

The next tab (if you have an active node tree) is **Preset** tab. This can be useful because it allows you to create your own personal library of custom nodes. We will talk about it in another chapter.

2.3.5. Properties region

Finally, we have the **properties** region. Here we can control settings and perform actions on selected nodes as well as on our node trees; plus, we can update Sverchok.

When you select a node, you will get three dedicated panels: *Node*, *Color* and *Properties*.
- In the **Node** panel you can set the *Name* and the *Label*. The **name** is what Sverchok uses internally to refer to that specific node and it must be univocal within the context of that node tree. The **label** is what appears on the header of the node and it doesn't have to be univocal. It is often a good idea to change the label of a node to make clear what it represents in the context of its tree. Underneath these two fields we have an area very useful if you want to

understand the functioning of a node. First of all you can check the **documentation** of the node **online, offline** or on **GitHub**. If you choose online you will be redirected to https://sverchok.readthedocs.io/en/latest/main.html, a resource that you can always check. Most of the nodes are described there, although not all of them and not all of them properly. In these cases, and not only in these cases, a good idea is to look directly at the source code of the node. You can do this easily with the next two buttons: *Edit source* externally and internally. Both of them will open the local files with the source code of the node, *Externally* on an external text editor that you specified in the settings of Sverchok (in the *User Preferences*, I use Visual Studio Code), *Internally* on the local Blender's text editor. Here you can look at the code of the node and really understand how it works. You can also modify it and save the changes, having your local custom version of Sverchok, but I don't recommend it.

- In the **Color** panel you can set the color of the node in the main area.

- In the **Properties** panel you will get the inputs of the node, plus in some cases, few more. Better to look at this area when you try a new node, you might find out some interesting **extra settings**.

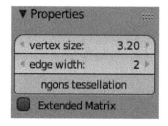

After these node specific one, we find some **generic panels**. The first and the second are dedicated to the **grease pencil**, and we can skip them.

- *SV. Import /export*; here you can import and export node trees. Node trees (or selected nodes) are exported in *json* format. You can then import such *json* files in the active node tree or in a new one. You can also import from a gist link, if you have the link saved in your clipboard . Create a folder dedicated to Sverchok and start to have there your own library or re-usable node trees.

- **Sverchok version panel**; in the header of this panel you can read your current version of Sverchok. If you want to update Sverchok you can click on **Check for updates**. If updates are available you will be asked if you want to update Sverchok. Remember to do this operation from time to time. To know what are the latest changes on Sverchok, click on **Show latest commits**. If new commits were pushed to GitHub they will appear in the *Info editor*. On the top of the panel you have two buttons for updating the current or all the node trees of the file. Sometimes you need to press them, if the auto-update gets frozen. Finally, a schematic view where you can control important aspects of your node tree; the *B* button allows you to bake all the nodes that have this possibility (like the `Viewer Draw`); the eye-icon button will hide the results of your node tree in the *3D view*; the *P* button is a very useful one. Sometimes your node tree can become heavy and updating it can take many seconds. In these cases you don't want the auto-update to run. You can disable it by clicking on this button. Now you can make the changes to you node tree that you want, and when you are ready you can reactivate the auto-update and click on *Update node tree*; the *F* button will make sure that your node tree is saved, even if it has zero users.

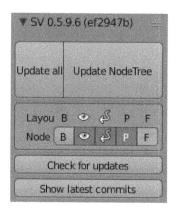

2.4 Debugging tools

One of the key competences that you need to acquire when learning a tool like Sverchok is **debugging**. It means to understand which parts of your parts of your program are producing errors or unexpected results. This is something that you will have to do much more often than you would like, especially at the beginning (but also later on). Let's see what are the main tools Sverchok offers to simplify this process.

2.4.1. Stethoscope, Viewer Text, Viewer Index

We have already talked about these nodes and we have already stressed their importance. They allow a **direct inspection** of the values of your lists of data. Thanks to them you can verify that both the content and the format (see nestedness level of input lists) of the data are correct. Use them often and use them wisely.

2.4.2. Logs

When a node produces a red error or it doesn't react and the direct inspection tools of the previous paragraph are not enough, an important help could come from the logs that Sverchok generates, where most of the times there are the informations that you need. To **see the Sverchok logs**, just select the file called "sverchok.log" from the *Text Editor*.

In the example below, for instance, we are passing a Float value to a socket that expects an Integer. In the log we can see that this is an error: "*TypeError: 'float' object cannot be interpreted as an integer*".

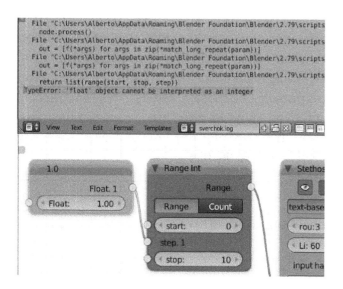

Sometimes we might need to look directly at the log produced by Blender, since some important information might not go to the Sverchok log. To **see the Blender's log**, in the *Info* editor, go to *Window* and select *Toggle System Console*. A new console window will open.

2.4.3. Heat map

Another useful tool is the *heat map*. This allows you to understand where are the **bottlenecks** of your node tree, meaning which are the nodes that are taking more time to compute. The nodes that take less time will be colored in white, while the slowest ones in red, with different gradations of pink in between.

In order to activate the heat map you need to go to the **Sverchok preferences** (inside the general Blender user preferences) and then under *General→Debug,* tick *Heat map.* Now close and reopen Blender and the heat map will be applied.

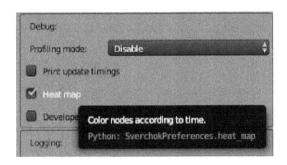

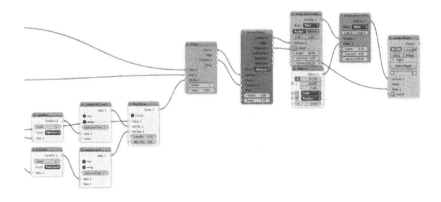

3. PROBLEM SETTING AND SOLVING IN COMPUTATIONAL DESIGN

How to approach the solution of a computational design problems? What are the steps that we have to take from start to finish? This will be the topic of the first part of the chapter. Later we will apply the knowledge that we've gained to solve a concrete task inside of Sverchok.

3.1 Problem setting

Now that we have a basic knowledge of Sverchok and its components, we can start to put together all the ingredients and apply them for our needs. That's what a tool like Sverchok and a programming language in general allows: it provides you with control and power, so that you can **produce results that would not normally be possible with standard and predefined tools**. I hope that by now you understood what the power of Sverchok is: by allowing you to access and **control directly, through mathematical operations, the individual vertices of a geometry**, you can generate all sort all things with it. In fact, although in Sverchok there are more than 150 nodes and counting, you could do almost everything with just a bunch of them, the basic ones, that we are covering in these first videos. All the other nodes are just adding layers of abstraction to facilitate actions that otherwise would require tens of nodes.

So you have some ideas, some projects that you would like to bring to life and you know that a parametric/computational method would be of big help. That's great, let's see the approach that we have to take when facing such projects. If you are new to programming and computational design, you have to learn to **think sequentially and to subdivide a problem in small steps**. Unlike "traditional" 3D modeling, where you can sketch something, change a little bit here, move it a little there, and what you do in one part of the model doesn't necessary affect what there is in another one, in computational design, although to some extent you can take a similar approach, at the end you will have to **come out with a coherent program** or node tree, where each node/function provides the correct inputs for the next one, until you reach the final output(s). Only at the end you will have time to play with all the parameters and sliders, when the whole structure (at least the main one) will be built and it will work like a clock. This is a different approach and for some of you at the beginning it may not be easy, as it was not for me as well when I started. Personally, I love it now. And I hope you will love it too.

When we are talking about programming, and it applies also to Sverchok, we need to distinguish between the solution of a problem and its implementation. The **solution** is the steps that we need to take to solve a particular problem and it can be expressed in general terms and in everyday language. The **implementation** is how we are going to translate the steps of our solution in the language of the tool we are using, in our case a Sverchok node tree. A common mistake is jumping to the implementation before having clear the solution. This should be avoided for all non-trivial problems.

There is rarely a single solution to a problem and there almost never is one single possible implementation of a solution. This leads us to the fact that there are good and bad (inefficient) solutions and good and bad implementations. Generally we want to create a solution that is: **correct** (obviously); **efficient** (takes only the necessary steps to accomplish the goal); **general** (can be used or adapted to solve a wider variety of situations. This last point is not crucial though). On the other hand, a good implementation is **efficient** (provides the desired output without waste of resources), **readable** (by other people and by yourself) and **maintainable** (for the future).

Let's see a **general strategy** that you could use when you are about to start a project in Sverchok, moving from the problem to the solution to the implementation:

1. **Have a vision of your final result:** what are you trying to achieve? What will your node tree do? How do you imagine it?

2. **Set the main goal:** from your general vision, identify the main goal that need to be achieved. It must be clear an minimal. Put aside every fancy and optional feature, you will work on them afterwards.

3. **Specify your inputs:** what are the main variables that will influence the result of your goal? If you want to create a grid, for example, your inputs could be the number of cells on the x,y axes.

4. **Identify the main steps to the solution:** now that you have the start and the end point, can you identify some clear sub-goals or sub-results that will lead you to the main one? If so, you can now treat each of them as a separate problem and apply the points of this list recursively. A good strategy to identify these steps is to **move backwards**, starting from the solution. Ask yourself: what is the last step before getting to the solution? Then repeat this question for what you have just found, and continue the process until you reach your input parameters.

5. **Review:** check your solution and verify if you are not taking any unnecessary steps. Can you think of a more efficient and straightforward way of reaching your goal? If the answer is no, move to the next point.

6. **Implement each step:** now that you have a clear path from the beginning to the end, you can start working on the implementation of each step. If you did the previous points correctly, this part will be fairly quick and fun.

7. **Test:** now you should have a working solution. Make sure that everything works correctly and that there are no bugs.

8. **Review and refactor:** look at your implementation and find the weak parts that could be more efficient. Also organize

your layout, make sure it's understandable. Tidy things up. Remember, a good implementation is efficient, readable and maintainable.

9. **Expand:** now that your main goal has been achieved, you can start to expand your node tree, adding more variables and functionalities, moving in the direction of the general vision that you had in the point number one. If an addition that you want to make is particularly complex, you can repeat the same process for that specific part.

10. **Enjoy your results!**

3.2 Drawing a square

3.2.1. Solution

Let's try to apply all these ideas in Sverchok now, starting from a small problem: **drawing a square**. Forget for now that under *Generators* there is the `Plane MK2` node that would allow us to do this in one shot. What we want is to create by ourselves the vertex list, the edge list and the polygon list and link them to the `Viewer Draw`.

Think by yourself now and come out with your own solution, following the steps that we have covered in the previous chapter, particularly the ones from one to five: how would you solve this problem? Which steps would you take? Which parameters would you use? Think in abstract terms and write you process on a piece of paper. Do it now.

Done it? As we said, there rarely is a single solution to a problem. We will now see one within the many available options. You can compare it with the one you wrote and decide which one is better.

As we know, the first thing that we need to have is a **clear goal**: we need the list of vertices, the list of edges and the list of polygons. Since edges and polygons depend on the vertex list, we will need to find this one first. This is our main goal.

What are the **main variables** that will influence our result? For sure we want to specify the size of the square and probably also its position. These will be our inputs.

How can we get the vertex list starting from our inputs? A common **strategy** for this problem is to specify the coordinates of the top-left vertex of the square and the length of its side and derive the other vertices from these two informations.

Given *(x,y)* the top-left vertex, where x is its position on the X axis and y its position on the Y axis and *l* the length of the side, the top right vertex will be *(x+l,y)*, the bottom right vertex will be *(x+l, y-l)*, the bottom left vertex will be *(x,y-l)*. Try to verify this on a piece of paper before continuing. After having all the vertices it will be easy to create the list of the 4 edges and the list of polygons (only one). Now we can move to the implementation in Sverchok.

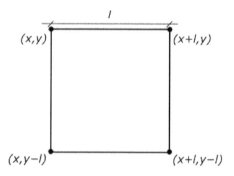

3.2.2. Implementation

Set up the input and output nodes first. Add a `Viewer Draw`, from *Number*, a `float` node and from *Vector* a `Vector in` node. Change the label of `float` to *Size* and the one of `Vector in` to *Top-left corner*. This is a good practice because in this way we are always sure about what our nodes represent.

If you look back at our solution, you will notice that, to get our four vertices, **we only need four values**: *x* and *y,* which we know from our *Top-left corner* node, and *x+l* and *y-l.* Let's get them.

From *Vector*, add a `Vector out` node. This node takes a vector as input and returns its *xyz* components. Link it with *Top-left corner.*

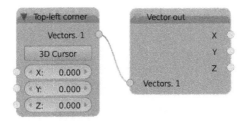

Now add two `Math MK2` nodes from *Number*, choosing the operator *Add* for one and *Sub* for the other; link to the *Add* node the X output socket of the `Vector out` and the *Size* value and to the *Sub* node the Y output socket and *Size* value.

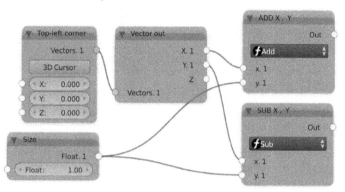

Now that we have the *(x+l)* and *(y-l)* points we can use `Vector in` to build the three other vertices of the square. As you can see from the screenshot for clarity I linked the X and Y sockets of `Vector out` to two `float` nodes and modified all the labels.

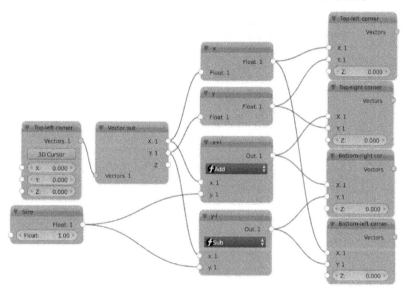

The last step is joining them in a single list for `Viewer Draw`. We can do it with the `List Join` node from *List→Main*. Keep a stable order (clockwise or counterclockwise) in the list and set the *JoinLevel lists* parameter to two, so that we can get a single object.

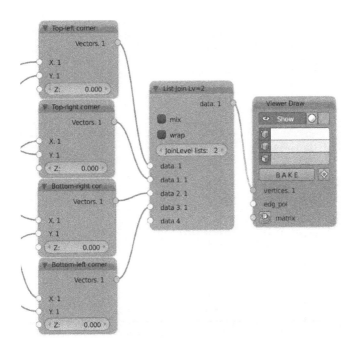

We now have the vertices and if we use the `Viewer Index` we can look at their indices. The final step is creating the edge list and the polygon list. Since we only have four edges we can write them directly. To do this we will use the `Formula` node, from *Number*. This is a handy node that allows us to write sequences of mathematical operations from different inputs. It can also create lists in place, what we will do now. Add two `Formula` nodes, look at the indices of the vertices and write the edge list and the polygon list.

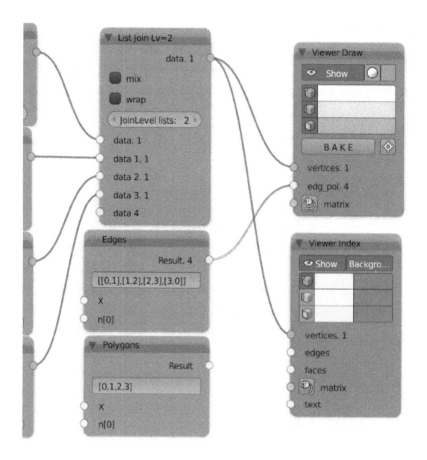

Great, now we have our square. For this specific case this solution is good. But what if we want to draw a triangle? Or an hexagon? Can we think to an approach that would allow us to draw all these polygons, only by specifying the number of sides? This will the topic of the next chapter, you can already start to think to a solution. But before, a couple of exercises.

3.2.3. Exercises

1. Create a node tree where you draw a square that has as input parameters its center's position and its length. You can follow the approach previously seen or go for a different path.

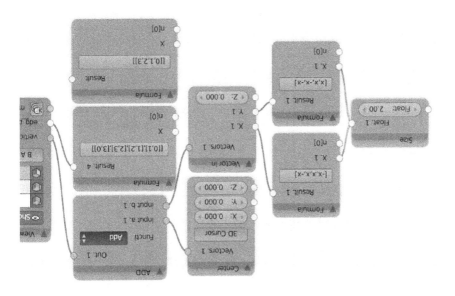

2. Adapt the two node tree created to draw squares so that they can draw also rectangles.

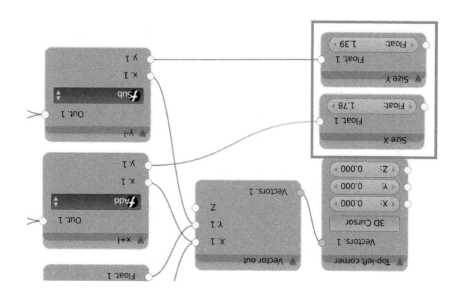

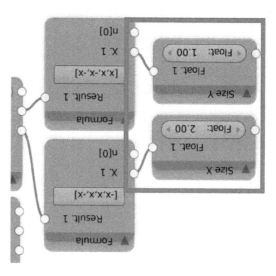

59

3.3 Drawing a regular polygon

In the previous chapter we have seen how to approach the solution of a computational design problem. We have used this knowledge to create a node tree that could draw a square starting from its top-left corner and its length and, in the exercise, from its center and its length. We have concluded that, although these solutions were effective, they were not general: in fact, if we want to use them to draw other regular polygons, like triangle or pentagons, we would have issues. In this chapter we will find a solution that will allow us to **draw any type of regular polygon**, by specifying only its number of sides.

3.2.1. Solution

Following our checklist from the paragraph 3.1 we can say that we want to create a node tree that generates regular polygons; the **main goal** will be finding the vertex list of such polygons; our **input parameters** will be the number of sides and the size of the polygon; to identify the **main steps** to reach our goal, we need to find some **common property** within the regular polygons that we can use for our purposes. It turns out that the solution lies in the definition of regular polygon itself: all regular polygons are *cyclic*(all corners lie on a single circle, called the circumcircle) and *equiangular*(all corner angles are equal). All we have to do to find the vertices of our polygon is to find the angle that separates its vertices lying on the circumference. We can then find their x,y position on the unit circle from the cosine and sine of the angle. Finally, we can scale the result by the desired length of the circumference. This will give us the vertex list, leaving us only to write the edge and the polygon list.

3.2.2. Implementation

Let's start by inserting the entry and exit points of our node tree. Add a Viewer Draw, a Float and an Int node. The Float will determine the final size of our polygon, the Int its number of sizes. We want to use an integer number because it doesn't make sense to have 4.34 sizes.

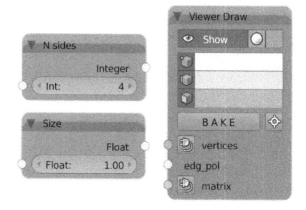

We can identify the angle that separates the vertices of the polygon lying on the circumference by dividing 2π by the number of sizes. We will use the two Math MK2 node for this purpose.

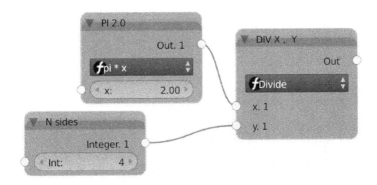

Now we want to know at what angle each vertex is on the circumference, starting from 0π. We will use the `Range Float` node from *Number* to generate this list. I suggest you to explore this node and understand its functioning because it's very useful and we will use it in many occasions.

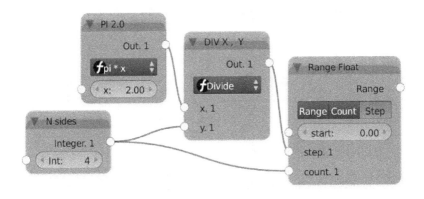

The nodes in the image above will produce the following list: [[0, 1.57, 4.14,4.71]]. To find the coordinates of the vertices we need to get the sine and cosine of these angles and multiply them by the size of our polygon (the radius of the circumference). Also, here we will use `Math MK2` nodes. Finally, we will plug the

62

results in a `Vector in` node and pass the created vertex list to the `Viewer Draw`.

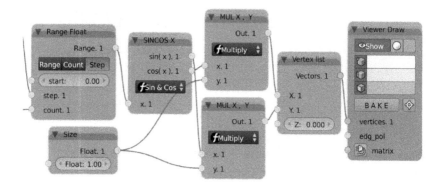

What we have left is the **edge list** and the **polygon list**. Unlike with the "draw a square" node tree created in the previous chapter, we cannot think now of manually writing the lists, since we can have a high number of sizes and since this number can always change. We need a way to **generate these lists automatically** simply from the *N sides* parameter. For this purpose, let's analyze the edge list written for the square:

`[[0,1],[1,2],[2,3],[3,0]]`

You can probably notice this pattern:

`[[0,1],[1,2],[2,3],[3,0]]`

The list going from 0 to the number of sides minus 1 is next to the same list shifted of one position. Let's try to reproduce this behavior in Sverchok.

First we will create the list going from 0 to the numbers of sides minus 1. We will use a `Range Int`, from *Numbers,* for this purpose. As *Stop parameter* you can either plug the *N sides* node or use `List Length` from *List→List Main* plugged with the vector list. The `List Length` node returns the number of elements inside a list.

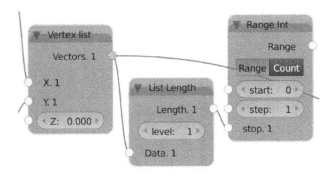

Now we need the second list, the one shifted by one element to the left. We have a node just for that, `List Shift` from *List→List Struct* that shifts the elements of a list at the specified level by the desired amount of positions, to the left or to the right. Experiment with this node and check the results in the `Stethoscope`.

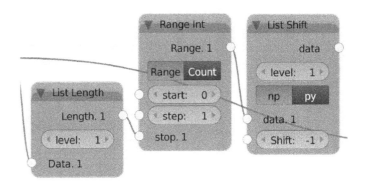

Now we will use a node, `List Zip`, from *List→List Main*, that takes two or more lists as inputs, then from each list takes every n^{th} element and creates a list out of them. For example, in our case we will have this, the edge list that we wanted:

$$[\ [\ 0, \ 1, \ 2, \ 3 \ ] \ ]$$

$$[\ [\ 1, \ 2, \ 3, \ 0 \ ] \ ]$$

$$[\ [\ [\ 0, \ 1 \ ], \ [\ 1, \ 2 \ ], \ [\ 2, \ 3 \ ], \ [\ 3, \ 0 \ ] \ ] \ ]$$

And the polygon list? Well, as you have probably already realized, it is the first Range Int node that we have already created:

$$[\ [0, \ 1, \ 2, \ 3] \ ]$$

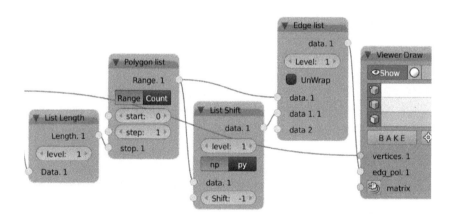

We have created a node tree that allow us to draw any type of regular polygon. What is we want to use it inside a bigger tree in the same or in another file? Should we copy and paste or export import all the nodes? It would not be practical. There is a way to

pack all of them together in a single node and add it to our **personal library**. We will talk about these possibilities in the next chapters.

3.2.3. Exercise

We have already tried a decent amount of nodes. Plus, we know the approach that we need to follow when facing a parametric design problem. Before moving forward, try to apply this knowledge and start making something your own. Have fun!

4. MONADS AND PRESETS

In this chapter we will see two useful Sverchok tools we can use to organize our node trees, making them more intelligible and faster do develop and reuse.

4.1 Monads

One of the features of Sverchok is the ability to create **node groups**, also known as **monads**, where you take a bunch of nodes and group them into a single one that has its own inputs and outputs.

4.1.1. Basics

Let's take for example the "Draw a polygon" node tree of the previous chapter. Since, of all the single nodes that we have used to create it, we can **abstract a single function** out of them - *draw a polygon* - we can actually create a single node with this purpose.

Practically speaking you want to **select all the nodes,** apart from the Viewer Draw (this is not mandatory but I think it's better to leave the nodes that render outside of the *Node Editor* out of the monads) and press *CTRL+G* or go to *Node→Make Group* in the *Node Editor header*.

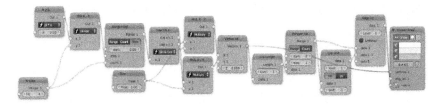

After pressing *CTRL+G*, the background of your main area will change to light green. You are now inside of the newly created monad.

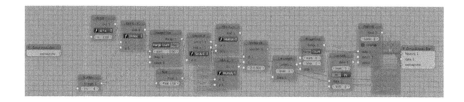

To get out of it, press *Tab* or click on *sv parent* on the left of the header of the *Node Editor*. You will see the node group you have just created.

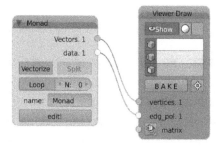

Before using it we still need to set up properly its input and outputs. Go again inside the monad (you can also click on *edit!*). We can link here our input parameters to *Group Inputs Exp* and the outputs to *Group Outputs Exp*.

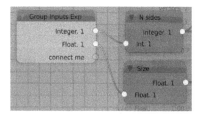

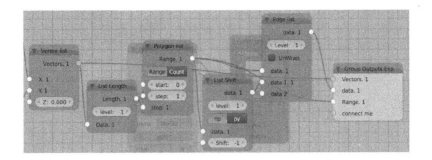

If now you open, inside the monad, the *properties' region*, you will see a new panel, *Sv Custom Group Interface*: here you can change the name of your inputs and outputs, set their order, their type as well as other settings like the default value. These changes will be reflected on input and output sockets of the group node.

We can now get out of the monad, change its label and start to use it as just any other node in Sverchok.

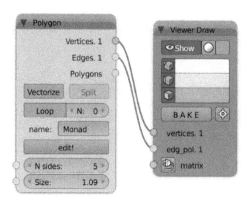

4.1.2. Vectorized monads

If you look at a group node, you will see that there is a button **Vectorize**. This offers you the possibility to **vectorize** our monad. Most of the nodes in Sverchok are vectorized, meaning that if we pass a vector of data (e.g. a list) they will perform their operations on each element of the list and they will output another list of the same length with the results. For example if we have a node that adds 1 to the input and we pass the list [5,4,1] we will get as output another list [6,5,2]. This is not obvious because some nodes can only process one element at the time and if we pass a list they will likely process only the first one and return just that, or none at all. If all the nodes inside a monad are already vectorized then the monad will be as well. But if one of them is not, then you will have to apply the *Vectorize* button to make sure that your monad can correctly process lists.

You can verify this with the *Polygon* monad itself. Try to pass a range of integers to the *N sides* parameter. Unless you vectorize (and here also *Split* to be sure that each input as length one) you

71

will get only one element as output, corresponding to the first element of the input list.

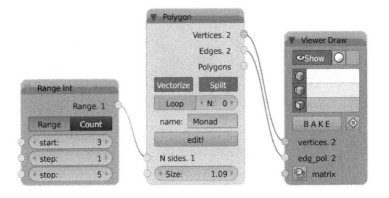

4.1.3. Monad loops

Another option that you see in the monad is the *Loop* parameters. This allows you to **cycle the data** of the monad, where the outputs of one loop become the inputs of the next one, until the specified number of repetitions is reached and the final result is provided.

The condition to use this feature is that the type and number of inputs and outputs have to be equal.

Here's for example how we can create a Fibonacci sequence (although there is already a specific node for that):

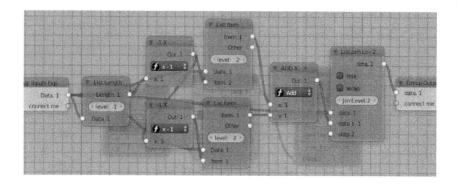

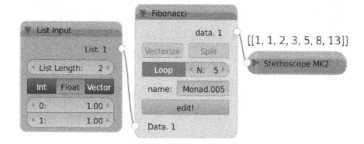

The maximum number of loops is by default limited to 5. If you want to increase this number, you can do it by going in the *Property region* inside of the monal to the *Sv Custom Group Interface*. Be careful though because in same cases you might get your computer stuck.

4.1.4. Duplicate monads

You can **duplicate monades** just like every other node (with copy/paste or with *SHIFT + d*). Just be aware that if you then modify a node group the changes will be applied also to the other duplicated monads. If instead you want to create a new independent monad from an existing one you need to right click on it and select *Make unique (Monad)*.

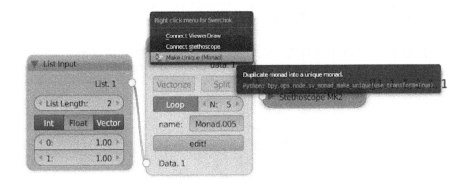

4.2 Presets

Presets allow you to save groups of nodes or monads into your own **personal Sverchok library** that you can reuse in any Blender file.

To access the *Presets* panel you need to open the *Tool shelf* of the *Node Editor*.

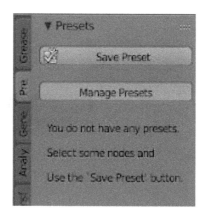

If now you select some nodes or a monad, for example the *Polygon* monad that we have created before, and click on *Save Preset,* you will be able to add it to your library that you can access from any Blender file.

Now when you will want to **use a preset** you will only have to click on its name in the *Presets* panel and it will be added to your current node tree.

Finally, if you click on **Manage Presets**, you can perform other operations, like import and export presets, edit metadata and delete them.

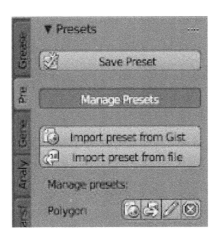

I encourage you to build your own library of presets and to make good use of it.

5. MATRICES

Matrices are a powerful tool that allows you to directly apply a set of transformations to an object. When I first started to learn Sverchok I was trying to avoid them because at the beginning they might not look so clear. Don't make this mistake and start to use them right from the start.

5.1 Matrices

5.1.1. Basics

As we already know matrices in Sverchok have a special type of socket, the blue one. If you link a matrix to a `Stethoscope` if you will see something different from usual:

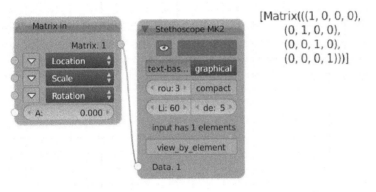

This is because a matrix is a **rectangular array** of numbers arranged in rows and columns. Matrices, through matrix multiplication, allow applying *linear transformations* to vectors. To apply a linear transformation in 3D we need a 4x4 (4 rows and 4 columns) matrix, which are the type that we see in Sverchok. If you know what you are doing or you want to experiment you can create directly a transformation matrix via the `Matrix Input` node from *Matrix*.

Matrix Input			
			Matrix
1.000	0.000	0.000	0.000
0.000	1.000	0.000	0.000
0.000	0.000	1.000	0.000
0.000	0.000	0.000	1.000

Anyway you don't need to get much into the mathematics behind matrices to use them effectively in Sverchok (although it's definitely useful to make some extra research on the topic by yourself). There are nodes that do the heavy lifting for you, in terms of creating a matrix and applying it to a list of vectors. The most common one is `Matrix in` from *Matrices*.

Try for example the following node tree and experiment in applying different values to the location (L), scale (S) and rotation (R) inputs.

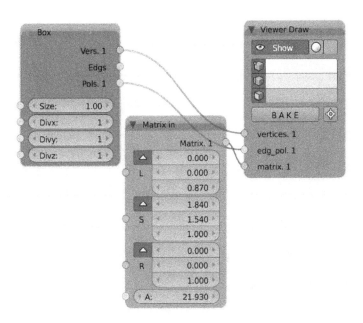

As you probably figured out already each vertex of the box will be added to the vector in *L*, it will be scaled for the vector in *S* and it will rotate *A* degrees around the axis going from (0,0,0) to *R*. In this way we can apply a **complex set of transformations** to an object in a single node. But it's not only that, since matrices are mathematical objects we can **manipulate**, for example we can interpolate between two matrices (Matrix Interpolation node), we can deform them (Matrix Deform node) or we can iterate over them to get interesting results (Iterate Matrix Transformation). Try to find all the matrix nodes inside of Sverchok (you can use the search option) and get familiar with them.

5.1.2. Lists of Matrices

Let's see something more that we can do with matrices. Try the following setup:

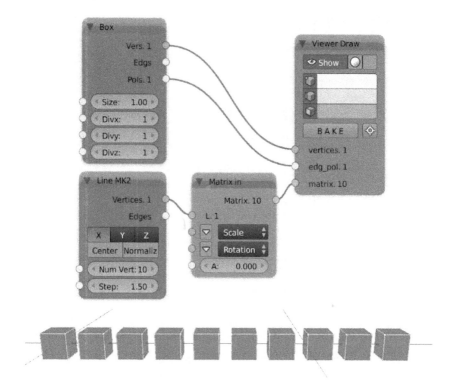

What happens is we get an object for each matrix that we have passed. In this way we can easily get arrays of objects with different properties starting from few inputs.

As a side note, please know that in Sverchok vectors can be read as location matrices and that the location component of a matrix can be read as vector.

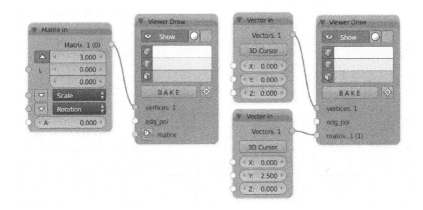

5.1.3. Matrix Apply

Finally, as you have noticed, until now we have seen the results of the matrix directly in the *3D view* by passing it to the Viewer Draw. We might need though to apply the transformation before, so that the changes are reflected on the values of the vertex list. We have two nodes for this: Matrix Apply from *Matrix* and Matrix Apply (verts) from *Transforms*. We use the first one when we want to apply the changes to a list of objects that have the vertex list and the edge/polygon list. We use the second one when we have only a list of vertices/vectors or a single object.

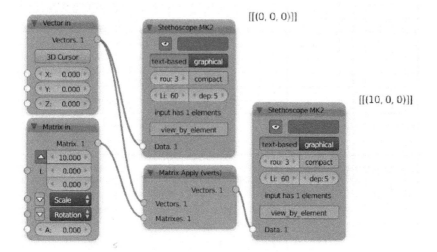

[[(0, 0, 0)]]

[[(10, 0, 0)]]

83

5.1.4. Exercise

Try to reproduce the following result.

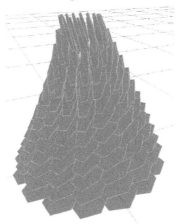

HINT: nodes you might want to use: NGon, Cylinder, List Length, Range Float, Vector in, Matrix in, Viewer Draw.

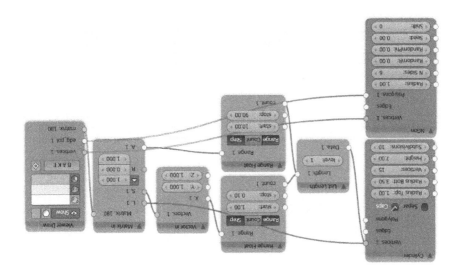

5.2 Twisting and object

We will now do an exercise that pretty much sums up what we have seen so far. We will have to set up the problem, make use of our knowledge of lists and debugging and use matrices. In the second part, to proceed, we will introduce another part of Sverchok relative to logic functions.

The exercise is twisting an object. Also here Sverchok already offers a node for that (`Simple deformation` from *Transforms*) but we are going to implement our own version.

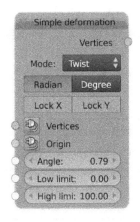

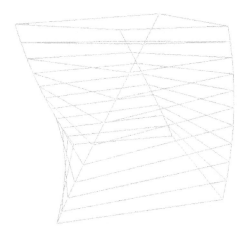

5.2.1. Problem setup

Let's take the `Simple deformation` node as a reference. There are few options and parameters available, however we understand the main ones are the *Vertices* and the *Angle*. These two are the two main inputs that determine the **core problem** that we are facing here, twisting an object. We need first to find a solution to this issue, starting from these two inputs and only after that we can add features to our node tree.

In order to find a solution to our problem we need to understand what is actually going one. "Twisting an object" gives us intuitively an idea of the final result but it's not descriptive of the causes. If we pay more attention, we will notice that what is happening is a **rotation of each vertex around the Z axis proportional to its z position**. This is what we have to achieve.

5.2.2. Implementation

If you remember we said that, when a problem is more complex, a good strategy is to **move backwards from its solution**. We now know that we need to apply different levels of rotations to each vertex. We also know that we can achieve this through matrices. The end of our node tree then will probably look something like this:

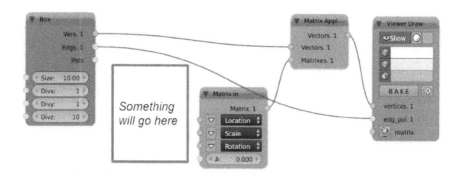

Keeping moving backwards, we know that the rotation depends on the z height of the vertices. We could then try the following approach:

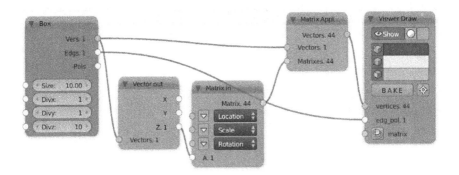

However, we see the result is not what we expect:

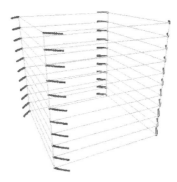

The reason for this behavior can be read in the `Matrix Apply` `(verts)` node. The *Vectors* list contains one object, while the *Matrixes* list contains 44 objects. Basically now we have created 44 vertex lists, each with each vertex rotated by the same amount. You can verify this in the `Viewer text`. What we want instead is one vertex list where each vertex is rotated by a different amount or, in other words, that each matrix is associated only with one vertex. The `Matrix Apply (verts)` node then needs to have the same amount of objects on both its input sockets. We can achieve this by splitting the vertex list of the `Box` in multiple lists, each containing only one vertex. Luckily we have a node that does just that and it's called `List Split`. If you plug it between the `Box` and the `Matrix Apply (verts)` you will already see the vertices rotating in the way expected. To control the result you can multiply the values that go the `Matrix in` node by a constant that you decide.

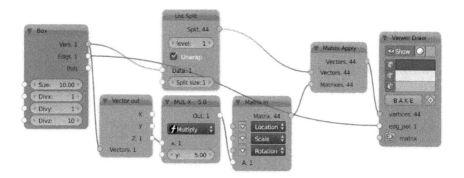

Finally, to see correctly the edges and the polygons of the box we need to join back all the vertices into a single list. We can do this with the `List Join` node and by setting the join level to 2.

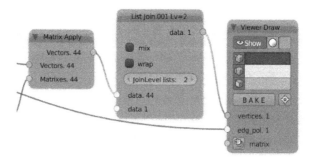

89

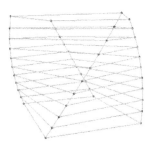

We have now reproduced the main features of a twisting node. If you look at `Simple deformation` we see we can also decide to filter out some vertices, starting from the bottom or from the top. It would be interesting to try to recreate also this part. To do so we need first to acquire some extra knowledge, in particular regarding logic functions and list masking inside of Sverchok. This will be the topic of the next chapter.

6. LOGIC

Being able to understand and use logic is a basic and essential skill in any programming language. Sverchok offers a set of tools that allow us to manage logic branches inside of our node trees and in this chapter we will see how to use them effectively.

6.1 Logic functions

6.1.1. Overview

We will start from the `Logic functions` node that you can find under the *Logic* category. When it comes to logic there are always only two possible results: *true* or *false*. True is represented with 1 and false with 0.

The `Logic functions` node provides a series of logic gates so that by giving the correct data we get results in the form of lists of true/false. If we want to check if a number is bigger that another one, for example we choose the greater than gate (> symbol) and we plug in the value that we want to compare in the *x* socket and the value that we want to compare against to in the *y* socket.

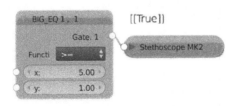

We can compare number or we can compare logic conditions. For example with the operator *And* we can verify if two conditions are both true. With the operator *Or* we can verify if at least one condition is true. With the operator *Xor* we can verify if only one condition is true.

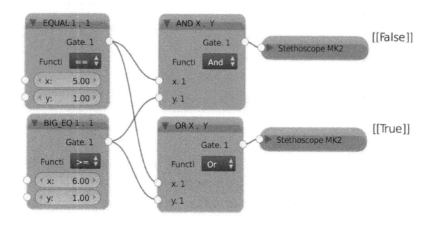

Experiment with all the logic functions and make sure to feel comfortable with them.

6.1.2. Exercise

In the previous chapter we have seen that, in order to implement the *Low limit* and the *High limit* parameters of the Simple deformation node for our twist-an-object node tree we need to check if a vertex's *z* value is within the two thresholds. Using logic functions create now a setup that can be later used in our node tree, where you check if a number is within two values.

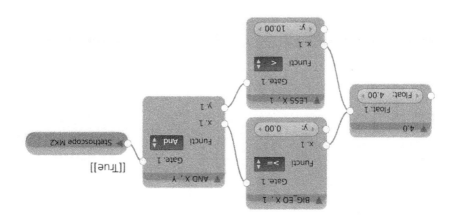

6.2 List masks

6.2.1. Overview

Let's assume that I have a list of number and that I want to multiply by two the even ones.

$$[1,2,3,4] \rightarrow [1,4,3,8]$$

With our current knowledge we should use some trick, like exploiting the fact the lists of true and false are just lists of 0 and 1 and that we can treat them as such:

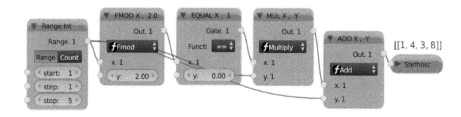

However, there is a better way, thanks to **list masks**. List masks are an extremely useful tool, since they allow us to filter the elements of a list and apply operations only to the desired ones. This can happen thanks to two nodes: List mask (out) and List Mask Join (in), both from *List*. Using these two nodes the previous example can be rewritten in the following way:

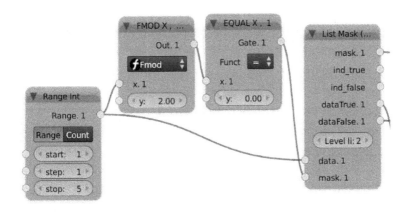

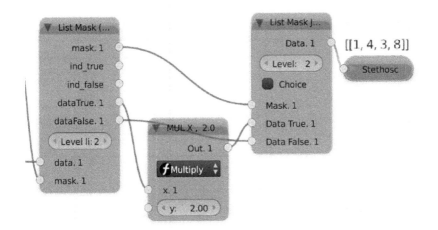

The List Mask (out) takes some *data* as input (it can be of any type) and a *mask*. A **mask** is a list of 0 and 1 (true and false, like the ones produced by the logic functions) of the same length of the *data* list. The node will then check which elements of the *data* list corresponds to a true value in the mask list and which value corresponds to a false. In our example the *data* list is [1,2,3,4] and the *mask* is [0,1,0,1] since we are checking for even numbers. The true values will then go in the *dataTrue* output socket and the false ones in *dataFalse* where they will be two new independent lists, in our example respectively [2,4] and [1,3]. We can now manipulate each of the two lists as we want. When we are done with the changes we can pass them to the List Mask Join (in), where we also provide the original *mask* (which for convenience we can take directly from List Mask (out)). As result we get again a single list with the values modified as we desired. Remember to set the correct *Level* in both nodes.

Some nodes already include list masks in the parameters like for example Extrude Separate Faces. In this case you just have to pass the mask list to the node.

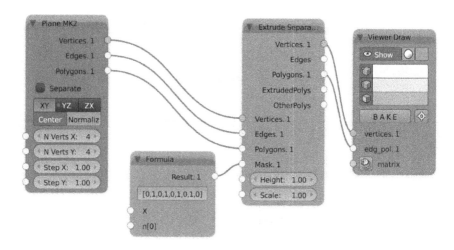

Make sure to practice and get comfortable with list mask since they are a great tool.

6.2.2. Exercise

Create a list of numbers from 0 to 100, check which values are between 25 and 75 and change into 1 those that are not.

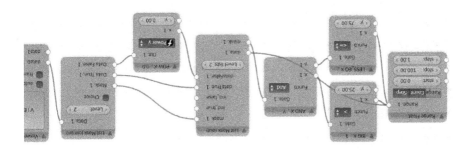

6.3 Twisting an object - part 2

6.3.1. Implementation

We now come back to our twisting node tree to implement the part relative to the **high and low limit**. What we need to do is to filter the vectors so that only those within the two threshold will be rotated. For this we will insert a mask before the `Matrix in` node.

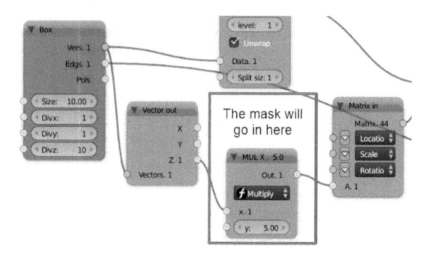

If you did the two previous exercise you already have a good idea of what we have to do now. In fact you could try to do it straight away. We will create two parameters for the high and low threshold, check which of the Z values are within the boundaries, apply to them the desired rotation and to those that are not a rotation of 0 (we will multiply the false values by 0), all thanks to list masks.

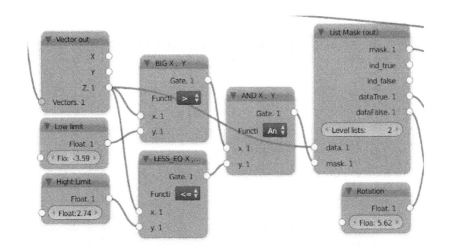

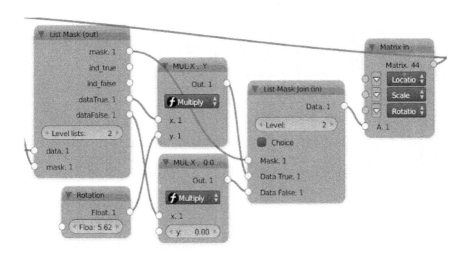

6.3.2. Exercise

If you compare the result of the previous paragraph with the one of the `Simple Deformation` node, you will notice that they are not identical. In the image below, on the left you have the result of our not tree, on the right the result of `Simple Deformation`.

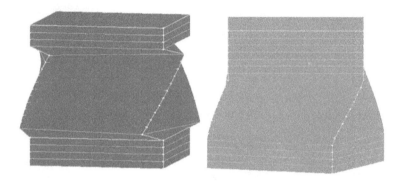

The `Simple Deformation` node gives a much more natural and harmonious result. First, try to understand **why this happens** and write it down.

What happens is that the rotation of the vertices that are not within the low and the high limit is the same of, respectively, the first and the last level of the vertices that are within the range.

Now try to **implement this solution** in Sverchok, expanding the node tree so far created. You might need to use a couple of nodes that we have not covered until now (especially from *List*) but I am sure that by now you are confident enough with Sverchok to look for and explore new nodes by yourself.

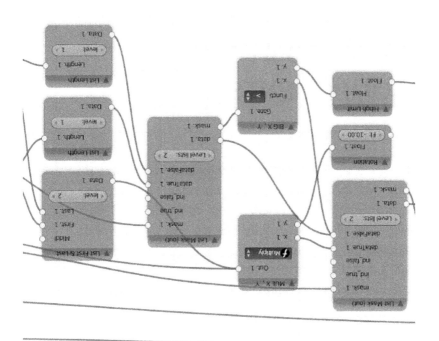

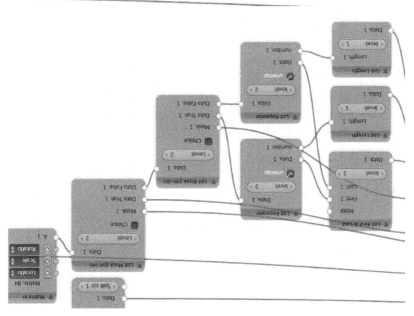

7. INTRO TO PYTHON COMPONENTS

In this chapter we will have a look at the tools that are available to expand the potential of Sverchok using Python, from few lines of code, until the skeleton of a new node. Since knowledge and application of Python are not goals of this book, this will be just a brief presentation for the readers that are interested in deepening the topic.

7.1 Formula

If you need to apply just few simple python functions, you can do this directly inside the `Formula node`, which we already know, from *Number*.

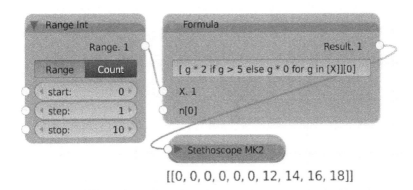

[[0, 0, 0, 0, 0, 0, 12, 14, 16, 18]]

7.2 Exec Node Mod

`Exec Node Mod` from *Number* is similar in capabilities to the `Formula node` but it offers more space and thus is better when you want to write slightly more complex functions. You will append the results to the `out` list which is already declared inside the node.

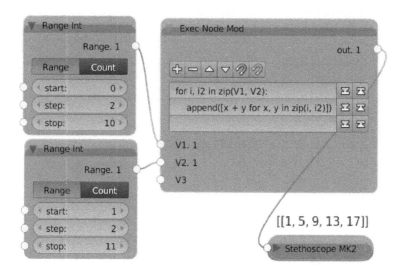

7.3 Scripted Node Lite

Together with the `Scripted Node`, this is one of the two ways inside of Sverchok to write complex custom nodes that look and behave just (or almost) like the default ones.

You will find the `Scripted Node Lite` under *Generator*.

The use is simple. First of all, in the *Properties* panel you will find a list of **templates** that you can use and refer to. Just click on *To Textblock* after you have selected one to see the content in the *Text Editor*.

If you want to create a **new script** from scratch, create a new text data-block in the *Text editor* and give it a name. Now you need to create a **header** for the script. The header will be included within a pair of triple quotation marks, like this:

```
"""

[HEADER HERE]

"""
```

In the header we will specify the input sockets and the output sockets. Once they are declared in the header, the sockets' names will automatically become variables available for the script. Here is a summary view of the header's syntax:

```
" " "
in  socketname type   default=x nested=n
out socketname type
" " "
```

We declare an **input socket** with `in`, then we specify its name, then its type (`v` for vertices, `s` for string and lists, `m` for matrices or `o` for objects, see also *2.2.3 Input and output sockets*).

We then provide a default value by writing `=` preceded by any character (you can write `default` or `d` or simply `.`) and then the default value itself (if it's a list we should not include any space within the iterable).

Finally, we specify the nestedness level. This is something you are familiar with since *2.1.6 Levels and objects*. Here is another explanation taken from the GitHub Sverchok repository[1]:

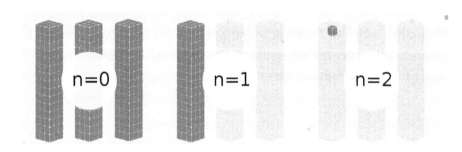

- `n=2` means `named_input.sv_get()[0][0]`

[1] https://github.com/nortikin/sverchok/issues/942

- o means you only want a single value.
- n=1 means `named_input.sv_get()[0]`
  - o You would use n=1 if you only ever plan to work with the first incoming sub-list. This will essentially ignore the rest of the incoming data on that socket.
- n=0 means `named_input.sv_get()`
  - o Generally you would use this if you plan to do something with each sub-list coming in, for example if the input contains several lists of verts like here:

So we could have for example:

```
in verts   v  d=[]   n=0
in radius  s  d=10   n=2
```

We declare the output sockets with `out` and then we write its name and type in the same way as for the input ones. For example:

```
out verts v
out edges s
```

After creating the header you can start writing you **python code** underneath it.

Once you have written the code, you can select your script from the drop-down list of the `Scripted Node Lite` and press on the **plug** icon. Your custom script will now behave like any other node.

The following is an example where, using Dijkstra's algorithm, we find the **shortest path** between two vertices on a mesh.

```
"""
in verts_in  v d=[] n=1
in edgs_in   s d=[] n=1
in idx_start      s d=0   n=2
in idx_target     s d=0   n=2
out verts    v
out edgs     s
"""

# Find the shortest path along a mesh
# See https://en.wikipedia.org/wiki/Dijkstra%27s_algorithm

neighbors = {}

for edge in edgs_in:
    for i in range(2):
        if edge[i] in neighbors:
            neighbors[edge[i]].append(edge[(i+1)%2])
        else:
            neighbors[edge[i]] = [edge[(i+1)%2]]

q = []
dist = []
prev = []

for i in range(len(verts_in)):
    q.append(i)
    dist.append( float("inf"))
    prev.append(None)

dist[idx_start] = 0

def length2(a, b, verts):
    v1 = verts[a]
    v2 = verts[b]
    return pow(v2[0] - v1[0],2) + pow(v2[1] - v1[1],2) +
pow(v2[2] - v1[2],2)



while len:
    dist_in_q = [ (x,i) for i, x in enumerate(dist) if i in q]
    u = min(dist_in_q, key = lambda t: t[0])[1]
    q.remove(u)
```

```python
        if u == idx_target : break

        for v in neighbors[u]:
            alt = dist[u] + length2(u,v,verts_in)
            if alt < dist[v]:
                dist[v] = alt
                prev[v] = u

u = idx_target

if prev[u] or u == idx_start:
    while u:
        verts.append(verts_in[u])
        u = prev[u]
else:
    print("Target not reachable")

if verts:
    edgs = [[[i, i+1] for i in range(len(verts)-1)]]
    verts = [verts]

print("Shortest path end ---- ")
```

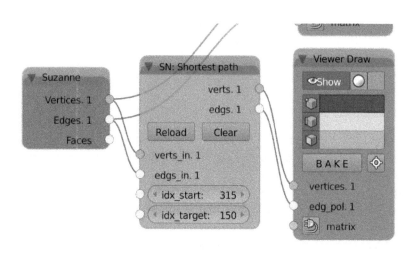

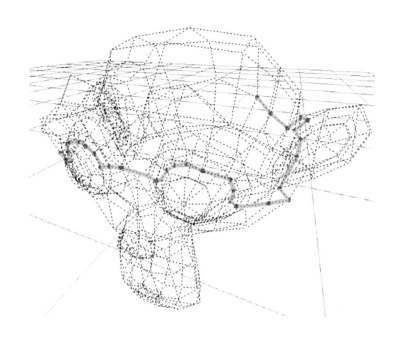

7.4 Scripted Node

The Scripted Node is similar to Scripted Node Lite, but it has a different setup system and has a couple of more functionalities.

You can find it under *Generator→Generator Extended*. Also in here there are various **templates** immediately available for use or as a start for further development.

The following part is partly taken from the online Sverchok Documentation:

To use the Scripted Node you must:
- Have one sv_main function as the main workhorse (but you can then define other functions/classes).
- sv_main must take at least one argument.
- All function arguments for sv_main must have defaults.
- Each script shall define in_sockets and out_sockets.
- ui_operators is an optional third output parameter.

The sv_main() can take ints, floats and lists or nested lists. For example:

```
def sv_main(vecs_in_multi=[[]], vecs_in_flat=[], some_var=1):
    pass
```

[[]] are for nested input (lists of lists);
[] for single (flat) lists;
int, float for single value inputs;

For **input and output sockets**:

```
in_sockets = [
    [type, 'socket name on ui', input_variable],
    [type, 'socket name on ui 2', input_variable2],
    # ...
]

out_sockets = [
    [type, 'socket name on ui', output_variable],
    [type, 'socket name on ui 2', output_variable2],
    # ...
]
```

- Each socket name on UI string shall be unique.
- Type are currently limited to vertices (`'v'`), strings and lists (`'s'`) and matrices (`'m'`).

The Scripted Node offers also the possibility to create *UI operators*, buttons that call a specific function of the script:

```
ui_operators = [
    ['button_name', func1]
]
```

- In the example, func1 is the function that will be called when pressing the button.
- Each "*button_name*" is the text that will appear on the button.

At the end of sv_main you will **return** either

```
return in_sockets, out_sockets
```

or

```
return in_sockets, out_sockets, ui_operators
```

Here is the shortest path example of the Scripted Node Lite, with highlighted the changes to adapt it to the Scripted Node. In particular, here we had to take care ourselves of the management of the nestedness of the lists.

```
# Find the shortest path along a mesh
# See https://en.wikipedia.org/wiki/Dijkstra%27s_algorithm

def sv_main(verts_in = [], edgs_in = [], idx_start = 0,
idx_target = 0):

    in_sockets = [
        ['v', 'in_vertices', verts_in],
        ['s', 'in_edges', edgs_in],
        ['s', 'idx_start', idx_start],
        ['s', 'idx_target', idx_target]
    ]

    def outSockets(v, e):
        return [ ['v', 'verts', v],['s', 'edgs', e] ]

    verts_in = verts_in[0] if verts_in else []
    edgs_in = edgs_in[0] if edgs_in else []

    if not verts_in or not edgs_in:
        return in_sockets, outSockets([],[])


    neighbors = {}
```

```
for edge in (edgs_in):
    for i in range(2):
        if edge[i] in neighbors:
            neighbors[edge[i]].append(edge[(i+1)%2])
        else:
            neighbors[edge[i]] = [edge[(i+1)%2]]

q = []
dist = []
prev = []

for i in range(len(verts_in)):
    q.append(i)
    dist.append( float("inf"))
    prev.append(None)

dist[idx_start] = 0

def length2(a, b, verts):
    v1 = verts[a]
    v2 = verts[b]
    return pow(v2[0] - v1[0],2) + pow(v2[1] - v1[1],2) +
pow(v2[2] - v1[2],2)

while len:
    dist_in_q = [ (x,i) for i, x in enumerate(dist) if i in
q]

    u = min(dist_in_q, key = lambda t: t[0])[1]
    q.remove(u)

    if u == idx_target : break

    for v in neighbors[u]:
        alt = dist[u] + length2(u,v,verts_in)
        if alt < dist[v]:
            dist[v] = alt
            prev[v] = u
```

```python
verts = []
edgs = []

u = idx_target

if prev[u] or u == idx_start:
    while u:
        verts.append(verts_in[u])
        u = prev[u]
else:
    print("Target not reachable")

if verts:
    edgs = [[[i, i+1] for i in range(len(verts)-1)]]
    verts = [[verts]]

print("Shortest path end ---- ")

return in_sockets, outSockets(verts, edgs)
```

FORWARD

I hope you found this book interesting and useful. If you want to contact me for anything, feel free to write to codeplastic@gmail.com and remember to check my blog www.codeplastic.com.

All the best.

A.G.

www.ingramcontent.com/pod-product-compliance
Lightning Source LLC
Chambersburg PA
CBHW070838070326
40690CB00009B/1604